1001 COOL JOKES

Published by Hinkler Books Pty Ltd 2013
45–55 Fairchild Street
Heatherton Victoria 3202 Australia
www.hinkler.com.au

© Hinkler Books Pty Ltd 2004, 2013

Illustrated by Glen Singleton
Cover design by Hinkler Books Design Studio
Cover illustration by Rob Kiely
Typeset by MPS Limited

ISBN: 978 1 7435 2070 3

Printed and bound in China

CONTENTS

Animals

1 **W**hat do you get when you cross an elephant with a fish?

Swimming trunks!

2 **W**hat happened when the dog went to the flea circus?

He stole the show!

3 **W**hat did the dog say when he was attacked by a tiger?

Nothing, dogs can't talk.

4 **H**ow did the skunk phone his mother?

On a smellular phone.

5   What do you get if you cross a cocker spaniel with a rooster and a poodle?

Cockerpoodledoo.

6   Why are four-legged animals bad dancers?

Because they have two left feet.

7   What do you call a woodpecker with no beak?

A headbanger.

8   What do you get when you cross a mountain lion and a parrot?

I don't know, but when it talks, you had better listen!

9   What do you get when you cross a chicken and a caterpillar?

Drumsticks for everyone!

10   What do you call a lamb with a machine gun?

Lambo.

11 **W**hat do you get when you cross a high chair and a bird?

A stool pigeon.

12 **W**hat do cats put in soft drinks?

Mice cubes.

13 **W**hat's 150 feet long and jumps every ten seconds?

A dinosaur with the hiccups.

14 **W**hat do you call a camel with three humps?

Humphrey.

15 **W**hat do you call a penguin in the desert?

Lost.

16 **W**hat do you get if you sit under a cow?

A pat on the head.

17 **W**hat do you call a duck with fangs?

Count Quackula.

18 **W**hat did Mr. and Mrs. Chicken call their baby?

Egg.

Isn't he gorgeous... Let's call him... EGG

19 **W**hat kind of tie do pigs wear?

A pigsty.

20 **W**hy don't turkeys get invited to dinner parties?

Because they use fowl language.

21 **W**hich side of the chicken has the most feathers?

The outside.

GOBBLE *@?!!X※ GOBBLE...GOBBLE

GOBBLE *@?!!X※
GOBBLE

22 **W**hat did the duck say when she finished shopping?

Just put it on my bill.

23 **W**hat do frozen cows do?

They give ice cream.

24 **W**hat is a dog's favorite food?

Anything that is on your plate!

25 **W**hat did the hen say when she saw scrambled eggs?

What a crazy mixed-up kid.

26 **W**hat do you get when you cross a rooster with a steer?

A cock and bull story.

27 **W**hy did the cow jump over the moon?

Because the farmer had cold hands.

28 **W**hy do mother kangaroos hate rainy days?

Because their kids have to play inside.

29 **W**hy did the chicken cross the basketball court?

He heard the referee calling fowls.

30 **W**hat do you call an elephant in a telephone box?

Stuck.

31 **W**hat do you call an elephant that never washes?

A smellyphant.

32 **W**hat do you give a sick elephant?

A very big paper bag.

33 **W**hat's black and very noisy?

A crow with a drum set.

34 **W**hy do elephants live in the jungle?

Because they can't fit inside houses.

35 **W**hy are elephants wrinkled all over?

Because they can't fit on an ironing board.

36   **W**hy are skunks always arguing?
Because they like to make a big stink!

37   **W**hat do you call a cow riding a skateboard?
A cow-tastrophe about to happen.

38   **W**hat do you get if you cross a parrot with a shark?
An animal that talks your head off!

39   **W**hy did the elephant paint the bottom of his feet yellow?
So he could hide upside down in custard.

40   **D**id you ever find an elephant in custard?
No.
It must work then!

41 **W**hat's black and white and eats like a horse?

A zebra.

42 **W**hat do get if you cross a centipede with a parrot?

A walkie-talkie.

43 **W**hat did the snail say when he hitched a ride on the turtle's back?

Weeeeeeeeeeeeeeeeeeeeee!!!!

44 **W**hat do you get if you cross a duck with a rooster?

A bird that wakes you up at the quack of dawn!

45 **D**id you hear the one about the dog running ten miles to retrieve a stick?

It was too far-fetched.

46 **W**hat's black and white and black and white and black and white?

A penguin rolling down a hill!

47 **W**hat do dogs and trees have in common?

Bark!

48 **W**hat is white, fluffy, and lives in the jungle?

A meringue-utan!

49 **W**hat's bright orange and sounds like a parrot?

A carrot!

50 **W**hat's tall, hairy, lives in the Himalayas and does 500 sit-ups a day?

The abdominal snowman!

51 **W**hat is a slug?

A snail with a housing problem.

52 **W**hat do you get if you cross a skunk with a bear?

Winnie the Poo.

53 **W**hat's the difference between an elephant and a flea?

An elephant can have fleas but a flea can't have elephants.

54 **D**id you know it takes three sheep to make a sweater?

Hmmm. I didn't even know they could knit.

55 **W**hat would you do if a bull charged you?

Pay him cash.

56 **W**hat steps would you take if a bull chased you?

Big ones.

57 **W**hat happened to the dog that swallowed the watch?

He got ticks.

58 **W**hy is the sky so high?

So birds won't bump their heads.

59 **W**hy do giraffes have long necks?

Because their feet stink.

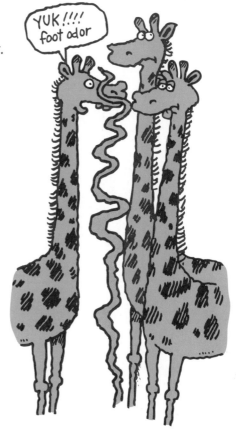

60 **W**hat's striped and goes around and around?

A zebra on a merry-go-round.

61 **W**here do bees go when they're sick?

To the waspital!

62 **H**ow do you milk a mouse?

You can't, the bucket won't fit underneath!

63 **W**hat time is it when you see a crocodile?

Time to run.

64 **W**hat time is it when an elephant sits on your fence?

Time to get a new fence.

65 **W**hat shouldn't you do when you meet a shark?

Go to pieces.

66 **W**hat do you call a baby whale?

A little squirt.

67 **W**hat are feathers good for?

Birds.

68 **W**hat do you get if you run over a sparrow with a lawn mower?

Shredded tweet.

69 **W**hat animal drops
from the clouds?

A raindeer.

70 **A**re you a
vegetarian because
you love animals?

*No, because I don't
like plants.*

71 **W**hy did they cross
a homing pigeon
with a parrot?

*So if it got lost it could
ask for directions.*

Lucky I brought my umbrella... its raining cats and dogs

72 **W**hat has four legs and
goes "Boo"?

A cow with a cold.

73 **W**hat do you call fourteen rabbits hopping
backwards?

A receding hareline.

74 **W**hy do gorillas have big nostrils?

Because they have big fingers.

75 **W**hat do you call a fly with no wings?

A walk.

76 **W**hat do you get if you cross a chicken with a yo-yo?

A bird that lays the same egg three times!

77 **W**hen is it bad luck to see a black cat?

When you're a mouse.

78 **W**hat's black and white and goes around and around?

A penguin caught in a revolving door.

79 **W**hy are elephants gray?

So you can tell them apart from canaries.

80 **W**hat do leopards say after lunch?

"That sure hit the spots!"

81 **W**hat did the canary say when she laid a square egg?

Ouch!

82 **W**hy did the dog cross the street?

To slobber on the other side.

83 **W**hat's the difference between a barking dog and an umbrella?

You can shut the umbrella up.

84 **W**hy are dogs like hamburgers?

They're both sold by the pound.

85 **W**hat did the duck say to the comedian after the show?

You really quacked me up!

86 **W**hy do birds fly south?

It's too far to walk!

87 **W**hat do you give a pig with a rash?

Oinkment!

88 **T**en cats were on a boat, one jumped off, how many were left?

None, they were all copycats!

89 **W**hy did the chicken cross the road?

To see the man laying bricks.

90 **W**hat's black and white and makes a terrible noise?

A penguin playing the bagpipes.

91 **W**hat's a pelican's favorite dish?

Anything that fits the bill.

92 **W**hat do you get when you cross an elephant with a sparrow?

Broken telephone poles everywhere.

93 **W**hat did Thomas Edison Elephant invent?

The electric peanut.

94 **W**ho went into the tiger's lair and came out alive?

The tiger.

95 **H**ow do you start a flea race?

One, Two, Flea, Go!

96 **W**hat do frogs order in restaurants?

French Flies!

97 **W**hy does a hummingbird hum?

It doesn't know the words!

98 **D**id you put the cat out?

I didn't know it was on fire!

99 **H**ow do you know that carrots are good for your eyesight?

Have you ever seen a rabbit wearing glasses?

The rabbit who wouldn't eat his carrots as a child...

100 **W**hat does a crab use to call someone?

A shellular phone!

a romantic table for two in the corner next to the large rock amongst the coral

101 What has four legs and sees just as well from both ends?

A horse with his eyes closed.

102 What do you call a sleeping bull?

A bulldozer!

103 What do you get when you cross a cat with a lemon?

A sour puss!

104 What kind of cat shouldn't you play cards with?

A cheetah!

105 Hickory dickory dock,

Three mice ran up the clock,

The clock struck one,

But the other two got away with minor injuries.

106 What do you give a dog with a fever?

Mustard, it's the best thing for a hot dog!

107 Why do cows wear bells?

Because their horns don't work!

108 What is gray, has big ears and a trunk?

A mouse going on vacation!

109   **W**hat did the porcupine
say to the cactus?

Are you my mother?

110   **W**hat happened to the snake with a cold?

She adder viper nose.

111   **H**ow can you stop
moles digging up
your garden?

Hide the shovel.

112   **W**hat's the difference between a unicorn and a
lettuce?

One is a funny beast and the other a bunny feast.

113 **W**hat would you get if you crossed a chicken with a mild-mannered reporter?

Cluck Kent.

114 **W**hat did Tarzan say when he saw the elephants coming over the hill?

Here come the elephants over the hill.

115 **W**hat is brown, has a hump, and lives in the North Pole?

A very lost camel!

116 **W**hat do you call a group of boring, spotted dogs?

101 Dull-matians!

117 **W**hy can't a leopard hide?

Because he's always spotted!

118 **W**hat did scientists say when they found bones on the moon?

The cow didn't make it!

119 **W**hat cat has eight legs?

An octopus.

120 **W**hat kind of dog tells time?

A watch dog!

121 **H**ow do you stop a rhino from charging?
Take away its credit card!

122 **W**hat do you call a pony with a sore throat?
A little horse!

123 **W**hat's the difference between a piano and a fish?
You can tune a piano, but you can't tuna fish!

124 **W**hat do you do with a blue whale?
Try to cheer him up!

125 **W**here do sheep go to get haircuts?
To the Baa Baa shop!

126 **W**hat looks like half a cat?
The other half!

127 **W**hy can't an elephant ride a tricycle?

Because they don't have thumbs to ring the bell!

128 **H**ow do you fit an elephant into a matchbox?

Take out the matches!

129 **H**ow do you fit a tiger into a matchbox?

Take out the elephant!

130 **W**hat is gray with sixteen wheels?

An elephant on roller skates!

131   **D**id you know that elephants never forget?
What do they have to remember!

132   **W**hy is a snail stronger than an elephant?

A snail carries its house, and an elephant only carries his trunk!

133   **W**hy is an elephant large, gray, and wrinkled?
Because if it was small, white, and smooth, it would be an aspirin!

134   **W**hat did one firefly say to the other before he left?
Bye! I'm glowing now!

135   **W**hy was the father centipede so upset?
All of the kids needed new shoes!

136 **W**hat do
you call a
mad flea?

A looney-tic!

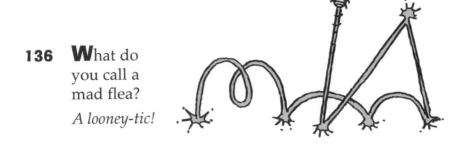

137 **W**hat kinds of bees fight?

Rumble Bees!

138 **W**hat are a bee's favorite soap operas?

The Bold & The Bee-utiful and Days of our Hives!

139 **W**hy was the bee's hair sticky?

Because he used a honey-comb!

140 **W**hy did the snail paint an S on its car?

So people would say, "Look at that S car go!"

141 **W**hat do you call two spiders who just got married?

Newlywebs!

142 **I**f a snake and an undertaker got married, what would they put on their towels?

Hiss and Hearse!

143 **W**hat are six things smaller than an ant's mouth?

Six of its teeth!

144 **H**ow do bees travel?

They take the buzz!

145 **H**ow do you make a snake cry?

Take away its rattle!

146 **W**hy did the firefly get bad grades in school?

He wasn't very bright!

147 **W**hat's worse than finding a worm in your apple?

Finding half a worm!

148 **W**here do you put a noisy dog?
In a barking lot!

149 **W**hat did the caterpillar say to the butterfly?

You'll never get me up in one of those things.

150 **W**hat do you call a
fly when it retires?

A flew.

151 **H**ow can you tell an elephant from a banana?

*Try to lift it up. If you can't, it's either an elephant or
a very heavy banana.*

152 **W**hat do you get when you cross an elephant with
peanut butter?

*Either an elephant that sticks to the roof of your mouth or
peanut butter that never forgets.*

153 **W**hat game do elephants play in a Volkswagen?

Squash!

154 **W**hat do
you call a monkey with a
banana in each ear?

Anything, he can't hear you.

155 **W**hy do tigers eat raw meat?

Because they can't cook.

156 **N**ow you see it, now you don't, now you see it, now you don't. What is it?

A black cat on a zebra crossing.

157 **W**hat is big, green, and has a trunk?

An unripe elephant.

158 **W**hat happened when the cow jumped over the barbed wire fence?

It was an udder catastrophe!

159 **W**hat do you call an unmarried female moth?

Myth.

160 **H**ow does an elephant get down from a tree?

He sits on a leaf and waits for fall.

161 **W**hat do you get from nervous cows?

Milk shakes.

162 What do you get if you cross an alligator with a camera?

A snapshot.

163 Why do elephants' tusks stick out?

Because their parents can't afford braces!

164 What's the biggest moth in the world?

A mam-moth.

165 What's the biggest mouse in the world?

A hippopotamouse.

166 What's green, wiggly, and goes "hith"?

A snake with a lisp.

167 **W**hy didn't the piglets listen to their father?
Because he was a boar.

168 **W**here can you buy ancient elephants?
At a mammoth sale.

169 **W**hy did the lion spit out the clown?
Because he tasted funny.

170 **W**hat did the beaver say to the tree?
It's been nice gnawing you.

NOW THAT'S A TASTY TREE!

171 **H**ow do you make toast in the jungle?
Put your bread under a gorilla.

172 **W**hat was the tortoise doing on the freeway?
About three miles an hour.

That's my funny bone!

173 **H**ow do tell which end of a worm is the head?
Tickle him in the middle and watch where he smiles.

174 **W**hat do you give a sick bird?
Tweetment.

175 **H**ow do you stop an elephant from smelling?
Tie a knot in his trunk.

176 **W**hat has two legs and two tails?

A lizard flipping a coin.

177 **H**ow do you hire a horse?

Put four bricks under his feet.

178 **W**hat should you know if you want to be a lion tamer?

More than the lion.

179 **W**hy did the fly fly?

Because the spider spied her.

180 **W**hat's bright blue and very heavy?

An elephant holding its breath.

181 **W**hat did the skunk say when the wind changed direction?

Ahhh, it's all coming back to me now.

182 **W**hy did the viper vipe her nose?

Because the adder 'ad 'er 'ankerchief.

183 **W**hat's the best way to catch a rabbit?

Hide in the bushes and make a noise like lettuce.

184 **W**hat goes 99 bonk?

A centipede with a wooden leg.

185 **W**hy do cows use the doorbell?

Because their horns don't work!

186 **W**hat's white
on the outside,
green on the inside,
and hops?

A frog sandwich.

187 **W**hat does a porcupine have for lunch?

A hamburger with prickles.

188 **W**hat do get when you cross a dog and a cat?

An animal that chases itself.

189 **H**ow can you tell
a rabbit from a
gorilla?

*A rabbit looks
nothing like a
gorilla.*

190 **W**hat did the goose say when he got cold?

"I have people-bumps!"

191 **W**hat lies down a hundred feet in the air?

A centipede.

192 **W**hat's the difference between a well-dressed man and a tired dog?

The man wears a suit, the dog just pants.

193 **W**hat lives at the bottom of the sea with a six gun?

Billy the Squid.

194 **W**hat did the mosquito say when he saw a camel's hump?

Gee, did I do that?

195 **H**ow many skunks does it take to stink out a room?

A phew.

196 **H**ow do goldfish go into business?

They start on a small scale.

197 **W**hy do snakes have forked tongues?

Because they can't use chopsticks.

198 **H**ow do you spell "mouse trap" with three letters?

C A T.

199 **W**hat did the dog say when he sat on the sandpaper?

Rough, rough!

200 **W**hat is more fantastic than a talking dog?

A spelling bee!

201 **W**hat do you get if you cross a giraffe with a porcupine?

A 30-foot toothbrush.

202 **W**hat can
go as fast as
a race horse?

The jockey!

203 **I**f horses wear shoes, what do
camels wear?

Desert boots.

204 **W**hy don't kangaroos ride bicycles?

Because they don't have thumbs to ring the little bell.

205 **W**hat's the same size and shape as an elephant but
weighs nothing?

*An elephant's
shadow.*

206 **W**hat's black
and white and
hides in caves?

*A zebra who
owes money.*

207 **W**here do you find a no-legged dog?

Right where you left it.

208 **H**ow do you get an elephant up an acorn tree?

Sit him on an acorn and wait twenty years.

209 **W**hat did one flea say to the other?

Shall we walk or take the dog?

210 **W**hat did the cat have for breakfast?

Mice Krispies.

211 **W**hat goes tick tick woof?

A watchdog.

212 **W**hy was the chicken sick?

Because it had people pox.

213 **H**ow do you get down from an elephant?

You don't get down from an elephant, you get down from a duck.

214 **W**hat do elephants have that no other animal does?

Baby elephants.

215 **W**hat's big, white, and furry, and found in outback Australia?

A very lost polar bear.

216 **W**hy do horses only wear shoes?

Because they would look silly with socks on.

217 **H**ow do you stop a pig from smelling?

Put a cork in his nose.

218 **W**hat's the difference between an African elephant and an Indian elephant?

About 3,700 miles.

Dinosaurs

219 **W**hat do you get if you cross a dinosaur with a vampire?

A blood shortage.

220 **W**hat do dinosaurs put on their french fries?

Tomatosaurus.

221 **W**hat's extinct and works in rodeos?

Bronco-saurus.

222 **W**hy did the dinosaur cross the road?

What road?

223 **W**hat do you call a
dinosaur with high
heels?

My-feet-are-saurus.

224 **W**hat do you get if you give a dinosaur a pogo
stick?

Big holes in your driveway.

225 **W**hat do you call a blind dinosaur?

Do-ya-think-he-saw-us?

226 **W**hat do you call a dinosaur that's a noisy sleeper?
Brontosnorus.

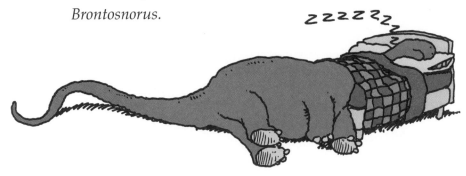

227 **W**hy did the baby dinosaur get arrested?
He took the bus home!

228 **W**hat's the best way to call a Tyrannosaurus Rex?
Long distance!

229 **W**hat does a Triceratops sit on?
Its Tricera-bottom!

230 **W**hat do dinosaurs put on their floors?
Rep-tiles.

231 **W**hat dinosaur can't stay out in the rain?

Stegosaur-rust!

232 **W**hat do you call a group of people who dig for bones?

A skeleton crew.

233 **W**hat do you get when a dinosaur skydives?

A large hole.

234 **W**hat has a spiked tail, plates on its back, and sixteen wheels?

A stegosaurus on roller skates.

235 **W**hat's the difference between a dinosaur and a sandwich?

A sandwich doesn't weigh five tons.

236 What's worse than a Tyrannosaurus with a toothache?

A Diplodocus with a sore throat!

237 Why couldn't the long-necked dinosaur see?

Because it had its head in the clouds!

238 What do you call a one-hundred-million-year-old dinosaur?

A fossil.

239 What do you get if you cross a dinosaur with a dog?

A very nervous mailman.

240 What's the difference between dinosaurs and dragons?

Dinosaurs are still too young to smoke.

241 **W**hat did the egg say to the dinosaur?
You're egg-stinct.

242 **W**hy didn't the dinosaur cross the road?
Because roads weren't invented.

243 **W**hat do you call a scared tyrannosaurus?
A nervous rex.

244 **W**hat dinosaur is home on the range?
Tyrannosaurus Tex.

245 **W**hy don't more dinosaurs join the police force?
They can't hide behind billboards.

246 **W**hat do you call
a dinosaur eating
a taco?

Tyrannosaurus Mex.

247 **W**hat do you call a dinosaur with magic powers?

Tyrannosaurus Hex.

248 **W**hat do you call a dinosaur that destroys
everything in its path?

Tyrannosaurus Wrecks.

Miscellaneous

249 **W**hy is six scared of seven?

Because 7-8-9.

250 **W**hat did the egg say to the whisk?

I know when I'm beaten.

251 **W**hat is scared of wolves and swears?

Little Rude Riding Hood.

252 **W**hy did the toilet paper roll down the hill?

To get to the bottom.

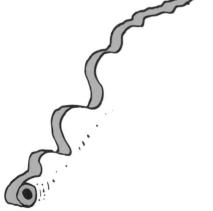

253 **W**hat's brown and sounds like a bell?

Dung.

254 **W**here are the Andes?

At the end of your armies.

255 **W**hat helps keep your teeth together?

Toothpaste.

256 **W**hat do you get if you cross a cowboy with a stew?

Hopalong Casserole.

257 **W**hat do you call a ship that lies on the bottom of the ocean and shakes?

A nervous WRECK!

258 **H**ow do you make a hotdog stand?

Steal its chair!

259 **W**hy was Thomas Edison able to invent the light bulb?

Because he was very bright.

260 **W**hat's the best way to win a race?

Run faster than everyone else.

261 **C**an a match box?

No, but a tin can.

262 **W**hy did the one-handed man cross the road?

He wanted to get to the second-hand shop!

263 **D**uring which battle was Lord Nelson killed?

His last one.

264 **W**hat did the floor say to the desk?

I can see your drawers.

265 Why did the surfer stop surfing?

Because the sea weed.

266 What was more useful than the invention of the first telephone?

The second telephone.

267 What's small, annoying, and really ugly?

I don't know, but it comes when I call my sister's name.

268 How do you use an Egyptian doorbell?

Toot-and-come-in.

269 **W**hat side of an apple is the left side?

The side that hasn't been eaten.

270 **H**ow can you tell a dogwood tree?

By its bark.

271 **W**hat invention allows you to see through walls?

A window.

272 **W**hat are the four letters the dentist says when a patient visits him?

ICDK (I see decay).

273 **H**ow did the dentist become a brain surgeon?

His drill slipped.

274 **W**hat's another word for tears?

Glumdrops.

275 **W**hich months have 28 days?

All of them.

276 **W**here does Tarzan buy his clothes?

At a jungle sale.

277 **H**ow do you make a fire with two sticks?

Make sure one of them is a match.

278 **W**hen do you put a frog in your sister's bed?

When you can't find a mouse.

279 **W**hy did Polly put the kettle on?

She didn't have anything else to wear.

280 **W**hat did the little light bulb say to its Mom?

I wuv you watts and watts.

281 **W**hy did the teacher wear dark glasses?

Because she had such a bright class.

282 **W**hy do toadstools grow so close together?

They don't need mushroom.

I just love dung for dinner

283 **W**hat did the judge say to the dentist?

Do you swear to pull the tooth, the whole tooth, and nothing but the tooth?

284 **W**hat happens when the Queen burps?

She issues a royal pardon.

EXCUSE ME!

Was it the beans, your Majesty?

285 **W**hat did one wall say to the other wall?

I'll meet you at the corner.

286 **W**here did the king keep his armies?

Up his sleevies.

287 **W**hy was the math book sad?

Because it had too many problems.

288 **W**hat's the letter that ends everything?

The letter G.

289 **W**hat did the stamp say to the envelope?

Stick with me and we will go places.

290 **W**hat do you call a man with an elephant on his head?
Squashed.

291 **I** have ten legs, twenty arms, and fifty-four feet. What am I?

A liar.

You can say that again!

292 **W**hat did the tie say to the hat?

You go on ahead, I'll just hang around.

293 **W**hat do you call a boomerang that doesn't come back to you?

A stick.

294 **W**here was the Declaration of Independence signed?

At the bottom.

295 **W**hy does lightning shock people?

It doesn't know how to conduct itself.

296 **W**hat did the pencil sharpener say to the pencil?

Stop going in circles and get to the point!

297 **W**hat's the nearest thing to silver?

The Lone Ranger's bottom.

298 **W**hat do Alexander the Great and Kermit the Frog have in common?

The same middle name!

299 **T**here are three kinds of people in the world. Those who can count. And those who can't.

300 **W**hat's the easiest way to get on TV?

Sit on it.

301 **W**hat has four legs and doesn't walk?

A table.

302 **W**here do you find giant snails?

At the ends of their fingers.

303 **N**ame three inventions that have helped man up in the world.

The elevator, the ladder, and the alarm clock.

304 **W**hat's brown, hairy, and has no legs but walks?

Dad's socks.

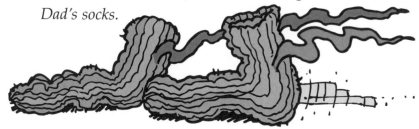

305 **H**ow do you saw the sea in half?

With a sea-saw.

306 **W**hat's easy to get into but hard to get out of?

Trouble.

307 **M**om, why isn't my nose twelve inches long?

Because then it would be a foot.

308 **D**ad, can you see a change in me?

No, why, son?

Because I swallowed twenty cents.

309 **H**ow did the rocket lose his job?

He was fired.

310 **W**hat's yellow and wears a mask?

The Lone Banana.

311 **W**hat has many rings but no fingers?

A telephone.

312 **W**hat do you get if you jump into the Red Sea?

Wet.

313 **W**hat's brown and sticky?

A stick.

314 **W**hat do you call a lazy toy?

An inaction figure.

315 **W**hy did the balloon burst?

Because it saw the soda pop!

316 **W**hat do all the Smiths in the telephone book have in common?

They all have telephones.

317 **W**hy do service stations always lock their bathrooms?

They are afraid someone might clean them.

318 **W**hat do you get if you cross the Atlantic with the Titanic?

About half way.

319 **W**hy did the bacteria cross the microscope?

To get to the other slide.

320 **W**hat do you do if your nose goes on strike?

Picket.

321 **W**hat's the hardest part about sky diving?

The ground!

322 **W**hat's the difference between a TV and a newspaper?

Ever tried swatting a fly with a TV?

323 **W**hat did the little mountain say to the big mountain?

Hi Cliff!

324 **W**hy did the traffic light turn red?

You would too if you had to change in the middle of the street!

325 **H**ow much does it cost for a pirate to get earrings?

A buccaneer!

326 **W**hat is the difference between a jeweler and a jailer?

A jeweler sells watches and a jailer watches cells!

327 **W**hat did the digital clock say to its mother?

Look, Ma, no hands.

328 **W**hy didn't the man die when he drank poison?

Because he was in the living room.

329 **W**hat do hippies do?

They hold your leggies on.

330 **W**hat did Snow White say while she waited for her photos?

Some day my prints will come!

331 **W**hat did one rain drop say to the other?

Two's company, three's a cloud.

332 **W**hat do you call a snowman with a suntan?
A puddle!

333 **W**hat did the penny say to the other penny?
We make perfect cents.

334 **W**hat did the Pacific Ocean say to the Atlantic Ocean?
Nothing. It just waved.

335 **W**ho was the smallest man in the world?
The guard that fell asleep on his watch.

336 **W**hat can jump higher than a house?
Anything, houses can't jump!

337 **W**hy did the bungy jumper take a vacation?
Because he was at the end of his rope.

338 **W**hy did E.T. have such big eyes?

Because he saw his phone bill.

339 **W**hat sort of star is dangerous?

A shooting star.

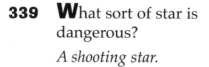

340 **W**hy did the belt go to jail?

Because it held up a pair of pants.

341 **W**hat is the name of the detective who sings quietly to himself while solving crimes?

Sherlock Hums!

342 **W**hy was the butcher worried?

His job was at steak!

343 **W**hat's the difference between an elephant and a matterbaby?

What's a matterbaby?

Nothing, but thanks for asking!

344 **W**hat did the shirt say to the blue jeans?

Meet you on the clothesline—that's where I hang out!

345 **W**hat did the big hand of the clock say to the little hand?

Got a minute?

346 **W**hat kind of music does your father like to sing?

Pop music.

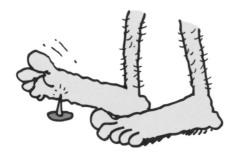

347 **W**hat's the easiest way to find a pin in your carpet?

Walk around in your bare feet.

348 **W**hat did the parents say to their son who wanted to play drums?

Beat it!

349 **W**here do you find baby soldiers?

In the infantry.

350 **C**an February
March?

*No. But
April May.*

351 **W**hat's the
definition of
intense?

*That's where
campers sleep.*

352 **W**hat do you
call a man who
stands around
and makes faces
all day?

A clockmaker.

353 **W**hat did one
toilet say to the
other toilet?

*You look a bit
flushed!*

354 **D**id you hear the one about the man who went into the cloning shop?

When he came out, he was beside himself!

355 **W**hat did the key say to the glue?

"You wanna be in show biz, kid? Stick to me, I can open doors for you!"

356 **W**hen does B come after U?

When you take some of its honey!

357 **W**hy was the archaeologist upset?

His job was in ruins!

358 **W**here does a sick ship go?

To the dock.

359 **D**id I tell you the joke about the high wall?

I'd better not, you might not get over it.

360 **W**hat did the first mind reader say to the second mind reader?

You're all right, how am I?

361 **W**hat did one ear say to the other ear?

Between you and me, we need a haircut.

362 **W**hat flowers grow under your nose?

Tulips.

363 **W**hat did the ear 'ear?

Only the nose knows.

364 **D**id you know that Davey Crockett had three ears?

A right ear, a left ear, and a wild frontier.

365 **W**hy does the ocean roar?

You would too if you had crabs on your bottom.

366 **W**hat will go up a drainpipe down, but won't go down a drainpipe up?

An umbrella.

367 **W**hat would you call superman if he lost all his powers?

Man.

368 **W**hat has a hundred legs but can't walk?

Fifty pairs of pants.

369 I have five noses, seven ears, and four mouths. What am I?

Very ugly.

370 What did one eye say to the other eye?

Something that smells has come between us.

Monsters

371 **L**ittle Monster: I hate my teacher's guts!

Mommy Monster: Then just eat around them!

You wouldn't like me if I start to cry...

372 **W**hat's green, sits in the corner, and cries?

The Incredible Sulk.

373 **W**hat's a vampire's favorite dog?

A bloodhound!

374 **W**hat do vampires cross the sea in?

Blood vessels.

375 **W**hat did the
alien say to the
gas pump?

*Take your finger
out of your ear
when I'm talking
to you.*

376 **W**hat did King Kong say when his sister had
a baby?

Well, I'll be a monkey's uncle.

377 **W**hy did the zombie decide to stay in his coffin?

He felt rotten.

378 **W**hat happened when the abominable snowman ate
a curry?

He melted.

379 **W**hat do you call a good-looking, kind, and
considerate monster?

A complete failure.

380 Little Monster: Should I eat my fries with my fingers?

Mommy Monster: No, you should eat them separately!

381 Mom, everyone at school calls me a werewolf.

Ignore them and comb your face.

382 What do sea monsters eat for lunch?

Potato ships!

383 Why did the cyclops give up teaching?

Because he only had one pupil.

384 Why do witches fly on broomsticks?

Because it's better than walking.

385 **W**hy did Dracula take some medicine?

To stop his coffin.

386 **W**hat do devils drink?

Demonade.

387 **W**hat don't zombies wear on boat trips?

Life jackets.

388 **W**hat do you call a sleeping monster who won't keep quiet?

Frankensnore.

389 **W**hat happened to Frankenstein's monster when he was caught speeding?

He was fined $50 and dismantled for six months.

390 **H**ow does a monster count to thirteen?

On his fingers.

391 **W**hat happened to the monster that took the five o'clock train home?

He had to give it back.

392 **W**hat kind of cheese do monsters eat?

Monsterella!

393 **W**hat do you get when you cross a vampire and a snowman?

Frostbite!

Aww, Mom, I hate my B-Negative cold!

394 **M**other vampire to son:

Hurry up and eat your breakfast before it clots.

395 **W**hat do you call a monster that was locked in the freezer overnight?

A cool ghoul!

396 **W**hat do you call a single vampire?

A bat-chelor.

397 **W**hat did the witch say to the vampire?

Get a life.

398 **W**hat do you get when you cross a skunk with Frankenstein?

Stinkenstein!

399 **W**hat do you call a ten-foot-tall monster?

Shorty!

400 **W**hat is a vampire's favorite kind of coffee?

De-coffin-ated!

401 **H**ow can you tell a Martian would be a good gardener?

They all have green thumbs!

402 **W**hat does a monster say when introduced?

Pleased to eat you.

403 **W**hat did the baby zombie want for his birthday?

A deady bear.

404 **W**hy did the sea monster eat five ships carrying potatoes?

Beacause you can't just eat one potato ship.

405 **W**hy doesn't anyone kiss vampires?

Because they have bat breath.

406 **W**hat do you think the tiniest vampire gets up to at night?

Your ankles.

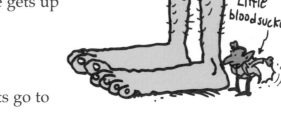

Little bloodsucker

407 **W**hy do ghosts go to parties?

To have a wail of a time.

408 **W**hy aren't vampires welcome in blood banks?

Because they only make withdrawals.

409 **W**hy do ghosts hate rain?

It dampens their spirits.

410 **W**hat time is it when a monster gets into your bed?

Time to get a new bed!

411 **W**hy did they call the Cyclops a playboy?

Because he had an eye for the ladies!

412 **W**hat does a ghost have to get before he can scare anyone?

A haunting license.

413 **W**hat did
one ghost say
to the other?

*Don't spook
until you're
spooken to!*

414 **W**hat do you call
a witch that lives
at the beach?

A sand witch!

415 **H**ow do you make a witch scratch?

Take away the W!

416 **W**hy do mummies have trouble keeping friends?

They're too wrapped up in themselves.

417 **W**hat do you get when a ghost sits in a tree?

Petrified wood!

418 **H**ow many witches does it take to change a light bulb?

Just one, but she changes it into a toad!

419 **W**ho is the best dancer at a monster party?

The Boogie Man!

420 **W**hat is a monster's favorite drink?

Ghoul-Aid!

421 **W**here does a ghost go on Saturday nights?

Somewhere he can boogie!

422 **W**hat is a spook's favorite ride?

A roller-ghoster!

423 **W**hat is the difference between a huge, smelly monster and candy?

People like candy!

424 **W**hat is Dracula's favorite fruit?

Necktarines!

425 **W**hat is Dracula's favorite place in New York?

The Vampire State Building!

426 **W**hat is a ghost's favorite dessert?

Boo-berries and I Scream!

427 **W**hy can't the Invisible Man pass school?

The teacher always marks him absent!

428 **W**hy did the monster eat the North Pole?

He was in the mood for a frozen dinner!

429 **W**hat is the best way to call Frankenstein's monster?

Long distance!

430 **W**hat is a ghost's favorite bedtime story?

Little Boo Peep!

431 **W**hat kind of mistake does a ghost make?

A boo-boo!

432 **W**hy do they have a fence around the graveyard?

Everyone is dying to get in!

433 **W**hat is big, hairy, and bounces up and down?

A monster on a pogo stick!

434 **W**hat is a ghost's favorite type of fruit?

Boo-berry!

435 **W**hat did the vampire say when he had bitten someone?

It's been nice gnawing you!

436 **W**hat did the skeleton say to the twin witches?

Which witch is which?

437 **W**hy is the vampire so unpopular?

Because he is a pain in the neck!

438 **W**hat does a ghost do when he gets in a car?

Puts his sheet belt on!

439 **W**hy didn't the ghost eat liver?

He didn't have the stomach for it!

440 **W**hat did the baby monster say to his babysitter?

I want my mummy!

MUMMMY!

Hold onto your hats, girls, while I try to turn this old stick into a stretch limo!

441 **W**hat do you call five witches on a broom?

A car pool!

442 **W**hy did Dr. Jekyll cross the road?

To get to the other Hyde!

443 **W**hat kind of fur do you get from a werewolf?

As fur away as you can get!

444 **W**ho did the monster take to the Halloween dance?

His ghoul friend!

445 **W**hy did Godzilla get a ticket?

He ran through a stomp sign!

446 **W**hat do you call a monster sleeping in a chandelier?

A light sleeper.

447 **W**hat is a mummy's favorite kind of music?

Rap!

448 **W**hat kind of boots do spooks wear?

Ghoulashes!

449 **W**here do ghosts live?

On dead ends!

450 **W**hy are ghosts such terrible liars?

Because you can see right through them.

451 **W**hat's a skeleton?

Someone with their outside off and their insides out.

452 **W**hat do you call a dumb skeleton?

A numbskull.

453 **W**hat kind of witch turns out the lights?

A Light-witch!

454 **W**hat did one skeleton say to the other?

If we had any guts, we'd get out of here!

455 **W**hat do you call a
vampire's dog?

A Blood Hound!

456 **H**ow do you know when a ghost
is sad?

He says Booooooooo Hooooooooo!

I hate those sad movies where the ghost gets exorcised.

457 **W**hat do
you do with
a green
monster?

*Put him in a
paper bag till
he ripens.*

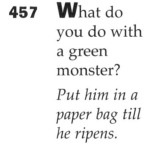

458 **D**id you hear about the ghost who ate all the
Christmas decorations?

He got tinselitis.

459 **W**hat do little ghosts
play with?

Deady bears.

460 **W**hat is Dracula's
favorite ice cream flavor?

Vein-illa!

461 **W**hy did the little monsters stay up all night?

They were studying for a blood test.

462 **W**hat do baby ghosts wear on their feet?

Booties!

463 **W**hy did the troll tell jokes to the mirror?

He wanted to see it crack up!

464 **W**hy do skeletons play the piano in church?

Because they don't have any organs!

465 **H**ow can you tell if a vampire has a cold?

He starts coffin!

466 **W**hat is a witch's favorite class in school?

Spelling!

467 **W**hat bear goes around scaring other animals?

Winnie The Boo!

468 **W**hat does a ghost read every day?

His horrorscope.

469 **W**here does Frankenstein's wife have her hair done?

At an ugly parlor.

470 **W**hat game do young ghosts love?

Hide and shriek.

471 **H**ow does an alien congratulate someone?

He gives him a high six.

472 **H**ow do monsters like their eggs?

Terrifried.

473 **W**hy couldn't the skeleton go to the dance?

He had no body to go with.

474 **W**hy didn't the skeleton cross the road?

Because he didn't have the guts to!

475 **W**hy did it take the monster ten months to finish a book?

Because he wasn't very hungry.

476 **H**ow many vampires does it take to change a light bulb?

None. They love the dark.

477 **W**hy are skeletons afraid of dogs?

Because dogs like bones.

478 **W**hat does a monster eat after he's been to the dentist?

The dentist.

479 **W**here do ghosts play golf?

At the golf corpse.

480 **W**hat do you call the winner of a monster beauty contest?

Ugly.

481 **H**ow do you make a skeleton laugh?

Tickle his funnybone.

482 **W**hat do witches put in their hair?

Scare spray.

HA HA HA

483 **W**hy are skeletons usually so calm?

Nothing gets under their skin!

484 **W**hat do ghosts eat for dinner?

Spook-etti.

I think the jeans are more you..

485 **W**hy don't skeletons wear shorts?

Because they have bony knees.

486 **D**o zombies have trouble getting dates?

No, they can usually dig someone up.

487 **W**hat does a boy monster do when a girl monster rolls her eyes at him?

He rolls them back to her.

488 **W**hat do you call a twenty ton two-headed monster?

Sir.

Doctor, Doctor

489 **D**octor, Doctor, I have a hoarse throat.

The resemblance doesn't end there.

490 **D**octor, Doctor, what is the best way to avoid biting insects?

Don't bite any.

491 **D**octor, Doctor, I feel like a tennis racket.

You must be too highly strung.

492 **D**octor, Doctor, my nose is running.

You'd better tie it up then.

493 **D**octor, Doctor, I'm afraid of the dark.

Then leave the light on.

494 **D**octor, Doctor, I keep stealing things.

Take one of these pills, and if that doesn't work, bring me back a computer.

495 **D**octor, Doctor, I feel like a pair of socks.

Well, I'll be darned.

Hey Doc...
Can I interest you in my complete boxed set?

496 **D**octor, Doctor, I think I'm a video.

I thought I'd seen you before.

497 **D**octor, Doctor I keep thinking I'm a yo-yo.

How are you feeling?
Oh, up and down.

498 **D**octor, Doctor, how can I stop my nose from running?

Stick your foot out and trip it.

499 **D**octor, Doctor, people keep disagreeing with me.

No, they don't.

500 Doctor, Doctor, I'm so ugly. What can I do about it?

Hire yourself out for Halloween parties.

501 Doctor, Doctor, I feel run down.

You should be more careful crossing the road then.

502 Doctor, Doctor, I'm at death's door.

Don't worry, I'll pull you through.

503 Doctor, Doctor, my stomach is sore.

Stop your belly aching.

504 Doctor, Doctor, I'm having trouble breathing.

I'll put a stop to that.

505 **W**hy do doctors wear masks?

Because if they make a mistake, the person won't know who did it!

506 **D**octor, Doctor, I feel like a dog!

Then go see a vet!

507 **D**octor, Doctor, I keep thinking I'm a doorknob.

Now don't fly off the handle.

508 **D**octor, Doctor, I'm a wrestler and I feel awful.

Get a grip on yourself then.

509 **D**octor, Doctor, some days I feel like a tee-pee, and other days I feel like a wig-wam.

You're two tents.

510 **D**octor, Doctor, I keep thinking I'm a dog.

How long has this been going on?

Ever since I was a pup.

511 **D**octor, Doctor, everyone hates me.

Don't be silly, not everyone has met you yet.

512 **D**octor, Doctor, I'm suffering from hallucinations.

I'm sure you are only imagining it.

513 **D**octor, Doctor, I feel like a piano.

Wait a moment, while I make some notes.

514 **D**octor, Doctor, will you treat me?

No, you'll have to pay like everybody else.

515 **D**octor, Doctor, I keep thinking I'm a $10 bill.

Go shopping, the change will do you good.

516 **D**octor, Doctor, I swallowed a spoon.
Well, try to relax and don't stir.

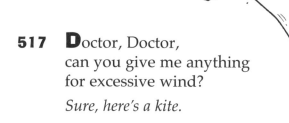

517 **D**octor, Doctor,
can you give me anything
for excessive wind?

Sure, here's a kite.

518 **D**octor, Doctor, I swallowed
a roll of film.

Don't worry, nothing will develop.

519 **D**octor, Doctor, I was
playing a kazoo and
I swallowed it.

*Lucky you weren't playing
the piano.*

520 **D**octor, Doctor, nobody
ever listens to me.

Next!

521 Doctor Doctor, I keep thinking I'm a joke.

Don't make me laugh.

522 Doctor Doctor, I'm turning into a trash can.

Don't talk such rubbish.

523 Doctor Doctor, I feel like an apple.

Well, don't worry, I won't bite.

524 Doctor, Doctor, I feel like a bell.

Well, take these, and if they don't work, give me a ring.

525 Doctor, Doctor, I'm as sick as a dog.

Well, I can't help you because I'm not a vet.

526 **D**octor, Doctor, my eyesight is getting worse.

You're absolutely right, this is a post office.

527 **D**octor, Doctor, the first thirty minutes I'm up every morning I feel dizzy. What should I do?

Get up half an hour later.

528 **D**octor, Doctor, what does this X-ray of my head show?

Unfortunately, nothing.

529 **D**octor, Doctor, this ointment you gave me makes my arm smart!

Try putting some on your head.

530 **D**octor, Doctor, something is preying on my mind!

Don't worry, it will probably starve to death.

531 **D**octor, Doctor, I feel like a set of curtains.

Well, pull yourself together.

532 **D**octor, Doctor, I accidentally ate my pillow.

Don't be so down in the mouth.

Hold on... I think we've got a crossed line... I'll hang up and dial again

533 **D**octor, Doctor, I have a ringing in my ears!

Well, answer it.

534 **D**octor, Doctor, every time I stand up I see visions of Mickey Mouse and Pluto, and every time I sit down I see Donald Duck!

How long have you been having these Disney spells?

535 **D**octor, Doctor, it hurts when I do this!

Well, don't do that.

536 **D**octor, Doctor, my leg hurts. What can I do?

Limp.

537 **D**octor, Doctor, I snore so loudly I wake myself up!

Try sleeping in another room.

538 **W**hen do doctors get angry?

When they run out of patience (patients).

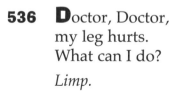

I think it might be the bait you've eaten

539 **W**hat do you call a surgeon with eight arms?

A doctopus.

540 **W**hy did the doctor tiptoe past the medicine cabinet?

Because she didn't want to wake the sleeping pills!

541 Doctor, Doctor, everyone thinks I'm a liar.

I don't believe you.

542 Doctor, Doctor, I feel like a pack of cards!

Sit down and I'll deal with you later!

543 Doctor, Doctor, I have a pain in the eye every time I drink hot chocolate!

Take the spoon out of your mug before you drink.

544 Doctor, Doctor, I only have 59 seconds to live!

Just a minute!

545 Doctor, Doctor, can you help me out?

Certainly—which way did you come in?

546 Doctor, Doctor, I dreamed that I ate a large marshmallow!

Did you wake up without a pillow?

547 Doctor, Doctor, I can't sleep at night!

Just lie on the end of your bed—you'll soon drop off.

548 **D**octor, Doctor, I'm invisible!

I'm sorry, sir, I can't see you right now.

NUT?

549 **D**octor, Doctor, my sister thinks she's a squirrel!

Sounds like a nut case to me.

550 **D**octor, Doctor, I think I'm getting shorter!

You'll just have to be a little patient.

551 **D**octor, Doctor, did you hear about the boy who swallowed a quarter?

No? Well, there's no change yet!

552 Doctor, Doctor, my son swallowed a pen. What should I do?

Use a pencil instead!

553 Doctor, Doctor, my wooden leg is giving me a lot of pain.

Why's that?

My wife keeps hitting me over the head with it!

554 Doctor, Doctor, my hair is falling out. Can you give me something to keep it in?

Yes, a paper bag.

555 Doctor, Doctor, I feel like I'm part of the internet!

Well, you do look a site.

556 Doctor, Doctor, I've been turned into a hare.

Stop rabbiting on about it.

557 Doctor, Doctor, I keep thinking I'm a dog.

Well, get up on this couch and I'll examine you.

I can't, I'm not allowed on the furniture.

558 Doctor, Doctor, can I have a second opinion?

Of course, come back tomorrow!

559 Doctor, Doctor, I feel like a window.

Where's the pane?

560 Doctor, Doctor, will my measles be better by next Monday?

I don't want to make any rash promises.

561 What did one tonsil say to the other tonsil?

Get dressed up, the doctor is taking us out!

562 Doctor, Doctor, I keep thinking I'm a fruitcake.

What's got into you?

Flour, raisins, and cherries.

563 Doctor, Doctor, you've got to help me, I keep thinking I'm a bridge.

What's come over you?

So far, a truck, a motorcycle, and two cars.

564 Doctor, Doctor, I keep hearing a ringing in my ears.

Where else did you expect to hear it?

565 Doctor, Doctor, what's good for biting fingernails?

Very sharp teeth.

Food

566 **W**aiter, you've got your thumb on my steak!

Well, I didn't want to drop it again.

567 **W**hy don't eggs tell jokes?

They'd crack each other up!

568 **W**hat did the banana sitting in the sun say to the other banana sitting in the sun?

I don't know about you, but I'm starting to peel.

569 **W**hat do you call a fake noodle?

An impasta.

570 **W**aiter, there's a fly in my soup!

Don't worry, sir, the spider in your salad will get it!

571 **W**hat is a cannibal's favorite soup?

One with a lot of body.

572 **W**hat did the raspberry say to the other raspberry?

We shouldn't have got into this jam.

573 **W**aiter, what is this fly doing in my soup?

Freestyle, I believe.

574 **H**ow do you fix a broken pizza?

With tomato paste.

575 **W**hat's yellow, brown, and hairy?

Cheese on toast dropped on the carpet.

576 **W**hat stays hot in the fridge?

Mustard.

577 **H**ow can you tell the difference between a can of soup and a can of baked beans?

Read the label.

578 **W**hat has bread on both sides and is afraid of everything?

A chicken sandwich.

579 **W**hat nut is like a sneeze?

A cashew.

580 **H**ey! There's no chicken in this chicken pot pie.

Well, do you expect to find dogs in dog biscuits?

581 **W**aiter, I'm in a hurry. Will my pizza be long?

No, it will be round.

582 **W**aiter, do you serve crabs in this restaurant?

Yes, sir, we serve anyone.

583 **W**aiter, this soup tastes funny.

Why aren't you laughing then?

584 **W**aiter, this apple pie is squashed.

Well, you told me to step on it because you were in a hurry.

585 **W**aiter, this egg is bad.

Well, don't blame me, I only laid the table.

586 **W**aiter, there is a small insect in my soup!

Sorry, sir, I'll get you a bigger one!

587 **W**hy is a pea small and green?

If it was large and red, it would be a fire engine.

588 **W**here do bakers keep their dough?

In the bank.

589 **W**hy did the potato cry?

Because the chips were down.

590 **W**aiter, there's a bug in my soup.

Be quiet sir or everyone will want one.

591 **W**hy did the baby cookie cry?

Because his mother was a wafer so long.

592 **W**aiter, do you have frogs legs?

No, I've always walked like this.

The secret to making great wine...

dirty feet

593 **W**hat do you get when you step on a grape?

A little wine.

594 **W**hat did the teddy bear say when he was offered dessert?

No thanks, I'm stuffed!

NO!... not even a little mint

595 **H**ave you heard the joke about the butter?

I'd better not tell you, you might spread it.

596 **T**wo sausages are in a pan. One looks at the other and says, "Gosh, it's hot in here", and the other sausage says,

"GOODNESS GRACIOUS, IT'S A TALKING SAUSAGE!"

Ahhr stop griping and just sizzle away quietly like the rest of us!

597 **M**om, can I have a dollar for the man who's crying in the park?

What's he crying about?

He's crying, "Hot dogs, one dollar."

598 **W**hat's the difference between pea soup and roast chicken?

Anyone can roast chicken.

599 **J**ohnny, I think your dog likes me, he's been looking at me all night.

That's because you're eating out of his bowl.

600 **W**hat's long, green, and slowly turns red?

A cucumber holding its breath.

601 **W**hat do you make from baked beans and onions?

Tear gas.

602 **W**aiter, how long will my sausages be?

Oh about 3 inches.

603 **H**ow do you fix a cracked pumpkin?

With a pumpkin patch!

604 **W**aiter, there's a fly in my soup.

Yes, sir, the hot water killed it.

605 **W**hy did the jelly wobble?

Because it saw the apple turnover.

606 **W**hat is red and goes up and down?

A tomato in an elevator!

607 **W**hy did the man at the orange juice factory lose his job?

He couldn't concentrate!

608 **H**ow do you make an elephant sandwich?

Well, first, you take an enormous loaf of bread . . .

609 **W**hy are cooks mean?

Because they beat the eggs and whip the cream!

610 **W**hy is a psychiatrist like a squirrel?

Because he's surrounded by nuts.

611 **W**hy should you never tell secrets in a grocery store?

Because the corn has ears, potatoes have eyes, and beanstalk.

612 **W**aiter, bring me something to eat and make it snappy.

How about an alligator sandwich, sir?

613 **W**hy did the cleaning woman quit?

Because grime doesn't pay.

614 **W**hy did the raisin go out with the prune?

Because he couldn't find a date.

615 **W**hy did Robin Hood rob the rich?

The poor didn't have any money.

616 **W**hat do you get if you cross a burglar with a cement mixer?

A hardened criminal.

617 **I**f I had six grapefruit in one hand and seven in the other, what would I have?

Very big hands.

618 **H**ow do you make a sausage roll?

Push it down a hill.

619 **W**hat did the cannibal have for breakfast?

Baked beings.

There goes your Father again!

620 **W**hat did the baby corn say to the mother corn?

"Where's pop corn?"

621 **W**hat did one plate say to the other plate?

"Lunch is on me!"

622 **W**hy did the baker stop making doughnuts?

Because he was sick of the whole business.

Gross

623 How do you make a hankie dance?

Put some boogie into it.

624 What is the soft stuff between a shark's teeth?

Slow swimmers.

625 Mommy, Mommy, can I lick the bowl?

No! You'll have to flush like everyone else.

626 Why are sausages so bad mannered?

They spit in the frying pan.

627 **W**hy are basketball players never asked for dinner?

Because they're always dribbling!

628 **W**hat's the difference between a maggot and a cockroach?

Cockroaches crunch more when you eat them.

629 **W**hat's green, sticky, and smells like eucalyptus?

Koala vomit.

630 **W**hat do you get if you cross an elephant with a box of laxatives?

Out of the way.

631 **W**hat is the difference between broccoli and boogers?

Kids don't like to eat broccoli!

632 **W**hy did Piglet look in the toilet?

He was looking for Pooh.

633 **W**hat do you find up a clean nose?

Fingerprints.

634 **W**hat's invisible and smells of carrots?

Bunny farts!!

635 **W**hat's the last thing that goes through a bug's mind when he hits a car windscreen?

His rear end.

636 **W**hy do little brothers chew with their mouths open?

Flies have got to live somewhere.

637 **H**ow do you keep flies out of the kitchen?

Put a pile of manure in the living room!

638 **W**hat's the difference between a worm and an apple?

Have you ever tried worm pie?

639 **H**ow can you tell when a moth farts?

He flies straight for a second.

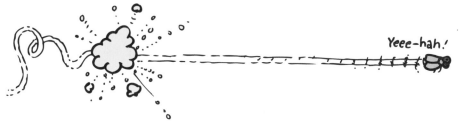

Yeee-hah!

640 **W**hat has two gray legs and two brown legs?

An elephant with diarrhea.

641 **W**hat makes you seasick?

Your little brother's vomit.

642 **W**hat is worse than finding a maggot in your apple?

Finding half a maggot!

643 **W**hat's another name for a snail?

A booger with a crash helmet.

644 **W**hat's yellow and smells of bananas?

Monkey vomit.

645 **W**hat's green and red and goes at 70 mph?

A frog in a blender.

646 **W**hat has fifty legs and can't walk?

Half a centipede.

WORLD LAND SPEED RECORD
ATTEMPT

Just Silly

647 How do you know when a doofus has been making chocolate chip cookies?

There are M&M shells on the floor!

648 How did the doofus fall on the floor?

He tripped over the cordless phone!

649 Why did the doofus break into two windows?

One to go in and the other to go out.

650 **W**hat's that on your shoulder?

A birthmark.

How long have you had it?

651 **W**hat happened to the doofus who couldn't tell the difference between porridge and putty?

All his windows fell out.

652 **W**hat did the farmer say when he lost his tractor?

"Where's my tractor?"

653 **W**hy did the doofus climb the glass wall?

To see what was on the other side!

654 **W**hy did the doofus get fired from the banana factory?

He threw out all the bent ones.

655 **W**hy was the doofus hitting his head against the wall?

Because it felt so good when he stopped!

656 **H**ow many fools does it take to screw in a light bulb?

Three . . . one to hold the bulb, and two to turn the chair!

657 How do you confuse a doofus?

Put him in a round room and tell him to sit in the corner!

658 How do you get a one-armed doofus out of a tree?

Wave to him.

659 What do you do if a doofus throws a hand grenade at you?

Pull the pin and throw it back.

660 What do you mean by telling everyone that I'm an idiot?

I'm sorry, I didn't know it was supposed to be a secret!

661 How can you tell when a doofus has been using the computer?

There is whiteout all over the screen!

662 What did the stupid burglar do when he saw a "WANTED" poster outside the police station?

He went in and applied for the job!

663 **H**ow do you keep a doofus in suspense?

I'll tell you tomorrow!

664 **H**ow did the doofus break his arm while raking leaves?

He fell out of the tree!

665 **W**hy did the doofus get fired from the M&M factory?

Because he threw away all the W's!

666 **W**hy did the doofus sleep under his car?

So he would wake up oily in the morning.

667 How do you sink a submarine full of fools?

Knock on the door.

668 Why was the fool's brain the size of a pea after exercising?

It swelled up!

669 What happened to the foolish tap dancer?

She fell in the sink.

670 Did you hear the one about the silly fox that got stuck in a trap?

She chewed off three legs and was still stuck.

671 **W**hy was the doofus covered in bruises?

He started to walk through a revolving door and then changed his mind!

672 **W**hat is the difference between a doofus and a shopping cart?

Shopping carts have a mind of their own.

673 **W**hy did the doofus go in the ditch?

Her turn signal was on.

674 **T**hree tourists were driving down the highway trying to get to Disneyland. They saw a sign that read:

"Disneyland Left." *So they went home.*

675 **H**ow do you know if a doofus sent you a fax?

There's a stamp on it.

676 **D**id you hear about the doofus who did bird impressions?

He ate worms.

677 **W**hy did the doofus leap out of the window?

To try his new jump suit.

678 **W**hy did the fool cross the road?

To get to the middle.

679 **W**hy did the fool put a chicken in a hot bath?

So she would lay hard-boiled eggs.

680 **H**ow do you make a doofus laugh on a Sunday?

Tell him a joke on Saturday.

681 **H**ow can you tell when there's a doofus on an oil rig?

He's the one throwing bread to the helicopters.

682 **W**hy did the doofus buy a chess set?

He was saving it for a brainy day.

683 **W**hat did the foolish ghost do?

Climbed over walls.

684 **W**hat happened to the stupid jellyfish?

It set.

685 **S**top! This is a one-way street!

Well, I'm only going one way!

686 **D**id you hear about the doofus who paid five dollars to have his thoughts read?

He got his money back.

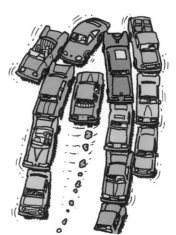

687 **W**hat did the doofus call his pet zebra?

Spot.

688 **D**id you hear about the doofus who got a boomerang for his birthday?

He spent the next two days trying to throw the old one away.

689 **D**id you hear about the bungee jumper who shot up and down for 3 hours before they could bring him under control?

He had a yo-yo in his pocket!

690 **W**hat's red and hangs in an orange tree?

A silly strawberry.

Silly Inventions

691 **A**n ejector seat on a helicopter.

692 **A** parachute that opens on impact.

693 **W**aterproof teabags.

You know... I've used this tea bag over 250 times... I think the secret's in the plastic coating

694 **A** left-handed screwdriver.

695 **A** one-way escalator.

Knock-Knock

696 **K**nock-Knock.
Who's there?
Cargo.
Cargo who?
Car go beep beep!

697 **K**nock-Knock.
Who's there?
Alison.
Alison who?
Alison to the
radio.

698 **K**nock-Knock.
Who's there?
Police.
Police who?
Police let me in.

699 **K**nock-Knock.

Who's there?

Gotter.

Gotter who?

Gotter go to the toilet.

700 **K**nock-Knock.

Who's there?

Mister.

Mister who?

Mister last train home.

701 **K**nock-Knock.

Who's there?

My panther.

My panther who?

My panther falling down.

702 **K**nock-Knock.

Who's there?

Aardvark.

Aardvark who?

Aardvark a million miles for one of your smiles!

703 **K**nock-Knock.

Who's there?

Caterpillar.

Caterpillar who?

Cat-er-pillar of feline society.

704 **K**nock-Knock.

Who's there?

Norma Lee.

Norma Lee who?

Norma Lee I'd be at school, but I've got the day off.

705 **K**nock-Knock.

Who's there?

Gladys.

Gladys who?

Gladys Saturday, aren't you?

706 **K**nock-Knock.

Who's there?

Witches.

Witches who?

Witches the way home?

707 **K**nock-Knock.

Who's there?

Lettuce.

Lettuce who?

Lett-uce in, it's cold outside.

708 **K**nock-Knock.
Who's there?
Tank.
Tank who?
You're welcome.

709 **K**nock-Knock.
Who's there?
Turnip.
Turnip who?
Turnip for school tomorrow or there will be trouble.

710 **K**nock-Knock.
Who's there?
Sawyer.
Sawyer who?
Sawyer lights on, thought I'd drop by.

711 **K**nock-Knock.
Who's there?
Freeze.
Freeze who?
Freeze a jolly good fellow.

712 **K**nock-Knock.

Who's there?

Turnip.

Turnip who?

Turn up the heater, it's cold in here!

713 **K**nock-Knock.

Who's there?

Scott.

Scott who?

Scott nothing to do with you.

714 **K**nock-Knock.

Who's there?

Robin.

Robin who?

Robin you! So hand over your cash.

715 **K**nock-Knock.

Who's there?

Roach.

Roach who?

Roach you a letter, but I didn't send it.

716 **K**nock-Knock.

Who's there?

Nanna.

Nanna who?

Nanna your business.

717 **K**nock-Knock.

Who's there?

Harley.

Harley who?

Harley ever see you anymore.

718 **K**nock-Knock.

Who's there?

Luke.

Luke who?

Luke through the
peephole and you'll see.

719 **K**nock-Knock.

Who's there?

Boo.

Boo who?

What are you crying about?

720 **K**nock-Knock.

Who's there?

Eiffel.

Eiffel who?

Eiffel down.

721 **K**nock-Knock.

Who's there?

Justin.

Justin who?

Justin time
for lunch.

I'm on a diet for my weight....

722 **K**nock-Knock.

Who's there?

Nobel.

Nobel who?

No bell so I just knocked.

723 **K**nock-Knock.

Who's there?

Minnie.

Minnie who?

Minnie people would like to know.

724 **K**nock-Knock.

Who's there?

Troy.

Troy who?

Troy as I may, I can't reach the bell.

725 **K**nock-Knock.

Who's there?

Kenya.

Kenya who?

Kenya keep the noise down, some of us are trying to sleep.

726 **K**nock-Knock.

Who's there?

Iran.

Iran who?

Iran 25 laps around the track, and boy, am I tired!

727 **K**nock-Knock.
Who's there?
Avon.
Avon who?
Avon you to open the door.

728 **K**nock-Knock.
Who's there?
Lionel.
Lionel who?
Lionel bite you
if you don't
watch out.

729 **K**nock-Knock.
Who's there?
Cows.
Cows who?
No, cows moo!

730 **K**nock-Knock.
Who's there?
Border patrol.
Border patrol who?
We ask the questions here!

731 **K**nock-Knock.
Who's there?
Ice cream!
Ice cream who?
Ice cream, you scream!

732 **K**nock-Knock.

Who's there?

Pencil.

Pencil who?

If you don't wear a belt, your PENCIL fall down!

733 **K**nock-Knock.

Who's there?

Tish.

Tish who?

Bless you!

734 **K**nock-Knock.

Who's there?

Shelby!

Shelby who?

Shelby comin' round the mountain when she comes!

735 **K**nock-Knock.

Who's there?

Dewayne!

Dewayne who?

Dewayne the bathtub before I drown!

736 **K**nock-Knock.

Who's there?

Midas.

Midas who?

Midas well let me in.

737 **K**nock-Knock.

Who's there?

Euripedes.

Euripedes who?

Euripedes pants, Eumenides pants.

738 **K**nock-Knock.

Who's there?

Miniature.

Miniature who?

Miniature let me in, I'll tell you.

739 **K**nock-Knock.

Who's there?

Arch!

Arch who?

Bless you!

740 **K**nock-Knock.

Who's there?

Max.

Max who?

Max no difference who it is—just open the door!

741 **K**nock-Knock.

Who's there?

Howard.

Howard who?

Howard I know?

742 **K**nock-Knock.

Who's there?

Red!

Red who?

Knock-Knock.

Who's there?

Red!

Red who?

Knock-Knock.

Who's there?

Red!

Red who?

Knock-Knock.

Who's there?

Red!

Red who?

Knock-Knock.

Who's there?

Orange!

Orange who?

Orange you glad
I didn't say red?

743 **K**nock-Knock.

Who's there?

Little old lady.

Little old lady who?

I didn't know you
could yodel!

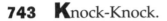

744 **K**nock-Knock.

Who's there?

Artichokes.

Artichokes who?

Artichokes when he eats too fast!

745 **K**nock-Knock.

Who's there?

Letter.

Letter who?

Letter in or she'll knock the door down.

746 **K**nock-Knock.

Who's there?

Tuba.

Tuba who?

Tuba toothpaste.

747 **K**nock-Knock.

Who's there?

Phyllis.

Phyllis who?

Phyllis a glass of water, will you?

748 **K**nock-Knock.
Who's there?
Still.
Still who?
Still knocking.

749 **K**nock-Knock.
Who's there?
Avenue.
Avenue who?
Avenue heard these jokes before?

I'll come back again tomorrow... and the day after too!

750 **K**nock-Knock.
Who's there?
Wayne.
Wayne who?
Wayne, wayne, go away, come again another day!

751 **K**nock-Knock.
Who's there?
Debate!
Debate who?
Debate goes on de hook if you want to catch de fish!

752 **K**nock-Knock.

Who's there?

Ben.

Ben who?

Ben knocking on the door all afternoon!

753 **K**nock-Knock.

Who's there?

Ammonia.

Ammonia who?

Ammonia (I'm only a) little girl who can't reach the door bell!

754 **K**nock-Knock.

Who's there?

Willube.

Willube who?

Willube my valentine?

755 **K**nock-Knock.

Who's there?

Water.

Water who?

Water friends for!

756 **K**nock-Knock.

Who's there?

William.

William who?

William mind your own business?

757 **K**nock-Knock.
Who's there?
Smore.
Smore who?
Can I have smore marshmallows?

758 **K**nock-Knock.
Who's there?
Arncha.
Arncha who?
Arncha going to let me in? It's freezing out here!

759 **K**nock-Knock.
Who's there?
M-2.
M-2 who?
M-2 tired to knock!

760 **K**nock-Knock.
Who's there?
The Sultan.
The Sultan who?
The Sultan Pepper.

761 **K**nock-Knock.

Who's there?

Waiter.

Waiter who?

Waiter minute while
I tie my shoe.

762 **K**nock-Knock.

Who's there?

Army.

Army who?

Army and you still friends?

763 **K**nock-Knock.

Who's there?

Wooden shoe.

Wooden shoe who?

Wooden shoe like to know.

764 Knock-Knock.

Who's there?

Wednesday.

Wednesday who?

Wednesday saints go marching in!

765 Knock-Knock.

Who's there?

Jamaica.

Jamaica who?

Jamaica mistake?

766 Knock-Knock.

Who's there?

Who.

Who who?

What are you—an owl?

767 Knock-Knock.

Who's there?

Ice cream soda.

Ice cream soda who?

Ice cream soda neighbors wake up!

768 **K**nock-Knock.

Who's there?

Shamp.

Shamp who?

Why, do I have lice?

769 **K**nock-Knock.

Who's there?

Empty.

Empty who?

Empty V (MTV).

770 **K**nock-Knock.

Who's there?

Vitamin.

Vitamin who?

Vitam in for a party!

771 **K**nock-Knock.

Who's there?

Despair.

Despair who?

Despair tire is flat.

772 **K**nock-Knock.

Who's there?

Icon.

Icon who?

Icon tell you another knock-knock joke. Do you want me to?

773 **K**nock-Knock.
Who's there?
House.
House who?
House it going?

774 **K**nock-Knock.
Who's there?
Closure.
Closure who?
Closure mouth
when you're
eating!

775 **K**nock-Knock.
Who's there?
Icy.
Icy who?
I see your
underwear.

776 **K**nock-Knock.

Who's there?

Tick.

Tick who?

Tick 'em up, I'm a tongue-tied towboy.

777 **K**nock-Knock.

Who's there?

Dishes.

Dishes who?

Dishes a very bad joke...!

778 **K**nock-Knock.

Who's there?

Weed.

Weed who?

Weed better mow the lawn before it gets too long.

779 **K**nock-Knock.

Who's there?

Alaska.

Alaska who?

Alaska one more time . . . let me in!

780 **K**nock-Knock.

Who's there?

Catch.

Catch who?

God bless you!

781 **K**nock-Knock.

Who's there?

Madam.

Madam who?

Madam foot got stuck in the door.

782 **K**nock-Knock.

Who's there?

Howdy!

Howdy who?

Howdy do that?

783 **K**nock-Knock.

Who's there?

Leaf.

Leaf who?

Leaf me alone.

784 **K**nock-Knock.

Who's there?

Butcher.

Butcher who?

Butcher little arms
around me!

785 **K**nock-Knock.

Who's there?

Stopwatch.

Stopwatch who?

Stopwatch you,re doing and open this door!!

786 **K**nock-Knock.

Who's there?

Winner.

Winner who?

Winner you gonna get this door fixed?

787 **K**nock-Knock.

Who's there?

Weirdo.

Weirdo who?

Weirdo you think you're going?

788 **K**nock-Knock.

Who's there?

Canoe.

Canoe who?

Canoe come out to play?

789 **K**nock-Knock.

Who's there?

Radio.

Radio who?

Radio not, here I come!

790 **K**nock-Knock.

Who's there?

Accordion.

Accordion who?

Accordion to the TV, it's going to rain tomorrow.

791 **K**nock-Knock.

Who's there?

Irish.

Irish who?

Irish I had a million dollars.

792 **K**nock-Knock.

Who's there?

Alex.

Alex who?

Alexplain later, just let me in.

793 **K**nock-Knock.

Who's there?

Zombies.

Zombies who?

Zombies make honey, zombies just buzz around.

794 **K**nock-Knock.

Who's there?

Cameron.

Cameron who?

Cameron a smile are all you need to take pictures.

795 **K**nock-Knock.

Who's there?

Abbot.

Abbot who?

Abbot you don't know who this is!

796 **K**nock-Knock.

Who's there?

Adore.

Adore who?

Adore is between us, open up!

797 **K**nock-Knock.

Who's there?

Sombrero.

Sombrero who?

"Sombrero-ver
the rainbow . . . "

eet eez such
a love-el-ly day.....
eet makes me want to sing!

798 **K**nock-Knock.

Who's there?

Alaska.

Alaska who?

Alaska no questions. You tella no lies.

799 **K**nock-Knock.

Who's there?

Irish stew.

Irish stew who?

Irish stew in the name of the law.

800 **K**nock-Knock.

Who's there?

Orson.

Orson who?

Orson cart!

801 **K**nock-Knock.

Who's there?

Felix.

Felix who?

Felix my ice cream, I'll lick his.

802 **K**nock-Knock.

Who's there?

Cornflakes.

Cornflakes who?

I'll tell you tomorrow, it's a cereal.

803 **K**nock-Knock.

Who's there?

Haywood, Hugh, and Harry.

Haywood, Hugh, and Harry who?

Haywood Hugh Harry up and open the door!

804 **K**nock-Knock.

Who's there?

Arthur.

Arthur who?

Arthur anymore jelly
beans in the jar?

805 **K**nock-Knock.

Who's there?

Theresa.

Theresa who?

Theresa green.

806 **K**nock-Knock.

Who's there?

Wilma.

Wilma who?

Wilma dinner be ready soon?

807 **K**nock-Knock.

Who's there?

Abbott!

Abbott who?

Abbott time you opened this door!

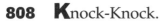

808 **K**nock-Knock.

Who's there?

Oscar.

Oscar who?

Oscar silly question, get a silly answer.

809 **K**nock-Knock.

Who's there?

Sancho.

Sancho who?

Sancho a letter, but you never answered.

810 **K**nock-Knock.

Who's there?

Celia.

Celia who?

Celia later alligator.

811 **K**nock-Knock.

Who's there?

Betty.

Betty who?

Betty late than never.

812 **K**nock-Knock.
Who's there?
Snow.
Snow who?
Snow good
asking me.

813 **K**nock-Knock.
Who's there?
Satin.
Satin who?
Who satin
my chair?

814 **K**nock-Knock.
Who's there?
Barbie.
Barbie who?
Barbie Q.

815 **K**nock-Knock.

Who's there?

Carrie.

Carrie who?

Carrie me inside, I'm exhausted.

816 **K**nock-Knock.

Who's there?

Irish.

Irish who?

Irish I knew some more knock-knock jokes.

Riddles

817 **W**hat are two things you cannot have for breakfast?

Lunch and dinner.

818 **W**hy did the boy throw butter out the window?

Because he wanted to see a butterfly!

819 **W**hat has eyes that cannot see, a tongue that cannot taste, and a soul that cannot die?

A shoe.

820 **W**hat can you hear, but not see, and only speaks when it is spoken to?

An echo.

821 **W**hat is there more of the less you see?

Darkness.

822 **W**hat ten letter word starts with gas?
A-U-T-O-M-O-B-I-L-E.

823 **H**ow many apples can you put in an empty box?
One. After that, it's not empty anymore.

824 **W**hen will water stop flowing downhill?
When it reaches the bottom.

825 **W**hat's black when clean and white when dirty?
A blackboard.

826 **W**hat's easier to give than receive?
Criticism.

827 **I**f April showers bring May flowers, what do May flowers bring?
Pilgrims!

828 **W**here can you always find a helping hand?

At the end of your arm.

829 **W**hy do firemen wear red suspenders?

To keep their pants up.

830 **W**hat kind of dress can never be worn?

Your address.

831 **W**hat weighs more—a pound of lead or a pound of feathers?

They both weigh the same.

832 **W**hat word is always spelled incorrectly?

Incorrectly.

833 **W**hat has a bottom at the top?

A leg.

834 **W**hy is milk the fastest thing in the world?

Because it's pasteurized before you see it.

835 **W**hat sort of ring is always square?

A boxing ring!

836 **W**hat's the last thing you take off before bed?

Your feet off the floor.

837 **W**hat starts with an "e", ends with an "e", and only has 1 letter in it?

An envelope!

838 **W**hat is always coming but never arrives?

Tomorrow.

839 **W**hat did the piece of wood say to the drill?

You bore me.

840 **W**hat can you serve, but never eat?

A volleyball.

841 **W**hat do you put in a barrel to make it lighter?

A hole.

842 **W**hat stays in the corner and travels all around the world?

A postage stamp.

843 **W**hat do you call a bee that is always complaining?

A grumble bee!

844 **W**hat's taken before you get it?

Your picture.

845 **W**hich room has no door, no windows, no floor, and no roof?

A mushroom!

846 **W**hat gets wet the more you dry?

A towel!

847 **W**hat's green, has eight legs, and would kill you if it fell on you from out of a tree?

A pool table.

848 **W**hat washes up on very small beaches?

Microwaves!

849 **W**hat breaks when you say it?

Silence!

850 **W**hat gets bigger and bigger as you take more away from it?

A hole!

851 **W**hat bow can't be tied?

A rainbow!

852 **W**hy are false teeth like stars?

They come out at night.

853 **W**hy do you go to bed?

Because the bed will not come to you.

854 **W**hat goes all around a pasture but never moves?

A fence!

855 **W**hat is H2O4?

Drinking!

856 **W**hat has teeth but cannot eat?

A comb!

857 **W**hat can you hold without touching?

Your breath.

858 **W**hat question can you never answer yes to?

Are you asleep?

859 **W**hat is the only true cure for dandruff?

Baldness!

860 **W**hat is big, red, and eats rocks?

A big red rock eater!

861 **W**hat goes all over the world but doesn't move?

The highway!

862 **W**hat starts with a P, ends with an E, and has a million letters in it?

Post Office!

863 **W**hat is always behind the times?

The back of a watch.

864 **W**hy can't it rain for two days in a row?

Because there is a night in between.

865 **W**hat goes up and does not come down?

Your age!

866 **W**hat was the highest mountain before Mt. Everest was discovered?

Mt. Everest.

867 **W**hat goes up and down but never moves?

A flight of stairs.

868 **H**ow many seconds are there in a year?

12 . . . 2nd of January, 2nd of February . . . !

869 **W**hich candle burns longer–a red one or a green one?

Neither, they both burn shorter!

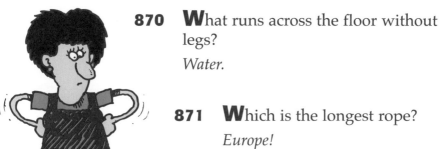

870 **W**hat runs across the floor without legs?

Water.

871 **W**hich is the longest rope?

Europe!

872 **W**hat has holes and holds water?

A sponge.

GO EASY!!

873 **W**hat puzzles make you angry?

Crossword puzzles.

874 **W**hat runs but doesn't get anywhere?
A refrigerator.

875 **W**hat do you call a superb painting done by a rat?
A mouseterpiece!

876 **W**hat kind of ship never sinks?
Friendship!

877 **W**hat has four fingers and a thumb, but is not a hand?
A glove!

878 **W**hat cup can you never drink out of?
A hiccup.

879 **W**hat kind of coat can you put on only when it's wet?
A coat of paint.

Are you sure you like it in lime green, full gloss?

880 **W**hat belongs to you but is used more by other people?
Your name.

881 **W**hat kind of cup can't hold water?
A cupcake.

882 **W**hat weapon was most feared by medieval knights?

A can opener.

883 **W**hen things go wrong, what can you always count on?

Your fingers.

884 **W**hat flies around all day, but never goes anywhere?

A flag.

LOOK... A POTATO

Where?

885 **W**here were potatoes first found?

In the ground.

886 **W**hat can you give away but also keep?

A cold.

887 **W**hat bet can never be won?

The alphabet.

888 **W**hat has two hands, no fingers, stands still, and runs?

A clock.

889 **W**hat is the beginning of eternity, the end of time, the beginning of every ending?

The letter "E".

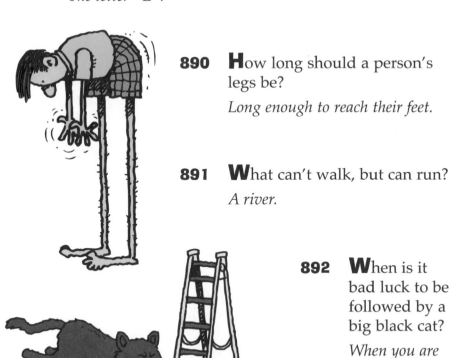

890 **H**ow long should a person's legs be?

Long enough to reach their feet.

891 **W**hat can't walk, but can run?

A river.

892 **W**hen is it bad luck to be followed by a big black cat?

When you are a little gray mouse.

Sport

893 **W**hy did the golfer wear two pairs of pants?

In case he got a hole in one.

894 **W**hat does every winner lose in a race?

Their breath.

895 **W**hy is a scrambled egg like the Bad News Bears?

They both get beaten.

896 **W**hat are the 4 seasons?

Baseball, basketball, soccer, and football!

897 **W**hat has 22 legs and two wings but can't fly?

A soccer team.

898 **W**here do old bowling balls end up?

In the gutter!

899 **W**hat illness do martial artists get?

Kung Flu.

900 **W**hat position did the pile of wood play on the football team?

De-fence!

901 **W**hen is a baby like a basketball player?

When he dribbles.

902 **W**hy was the boxer known as Picasso?

Because he spent all his time on the canvas.

903 **W**hy did the runner wear rippled sole shoes?

To give the ants a fifty-fifty chance.

904 **W**hat did one bowling ball say to the other?

Don't stop me, I'm on a roll.

905 **W**hat's a ghost's favorite position in soccer?

Ghoul-keeper.

906 **W**hat happens when baseball players get old?

They go batty.

907 **W**hy were the arrows nervous?

Because they were all in a quiver.

908 **W**hat do you get when you cross a football player with a gorilla?

I don't know, but nobody tries to stop it from scoring.

909 **W**hy did all the bowling pins go down?

Because they were on strike.

910 **W**hy do soccer players have so much trouble eating?

They think they can't use their hands.

911 **W**hy was the centipede two hours late for the soccer match?

It took him two hours to put his shoes on.

912 **W**hy are basketball players always so cool?

Because of all the fans.

913 **W**hy was the chickens' soccer match a bad idea?

Because there were too many fowls.

914 **W**hy is tennis such a noisy game?

Because everyone raises a racket.

915 **W**hy is Cinderella so bad at sport?

Because she has a pumpkin for a coach, and she runs away from the ball.

Computers

916 **W**hy was the computer so tired when it got home?

Because . . . it had a hard drive!

917 **W**here are computers kept at school?

On their desk drive.

918 **W**hat did the computer say when a man typed something in on the keyboard?

You're really pushing my buttons, little man!

919 **H**ow many programmers does it take to screw in a light bulb?

None, it's a hardware problem!

920 **W**here do you find the biggest spider?

In the world wide web.

921 **W**hy did the computer cross the road?

Because it was programmed by the chicken.

922 **W**hat do you get if you cross a computer programmer with an athlete?

A diskus thrower.

923 **H**ey, did you see who stole my computer?

Yes, he went data way!

924 **W**hy did the computer sneeze?

It had a virus.

925 **W**hat did the computer say to the programmer at lunchtime?

Can I have a byte?

926 **W**hat do computers do when they get hungry?

They eat chips.

927 **W**hat is the computer's favorite dance?

Disk-o.

What do you call...

928 . . . a man who likes to work out?

Jim!

929 . . . a girl with a tennis racket on her head?

Annette!

930 . . . a woman with a cat on her head?

Kitty!

931 . . . a woman with one leg?

Eileen!

932 . . . a boy hanging on the wall?

Art!

933 ... a man with a map
on his head?

Miles!

934 ... a man with a car
on his head?

Jack!

935 ... a man who owes
money?

Bill!

936 ... a man with a
spade?

Doug!

937 ... a man without
a spade?

Douglas!

938 ... a girl with a frog on
her head?

Lily!

939 ... a man in a pile of
leaves?

Russell!

940 ... a woman in the
distance?

Dot!

941 . . . a man with a Christmas tree on his head?

Noel.

942 . . . a woman with a Christmas tree on her head?

Carol.

943 . . . a lady standing in the middle of a tennis court?

Annette!

944 . . . a man with rabbits in his trousers?

Warren.

Silly Book Titles

945 "The Invisible Man" by Peter Out.

946 "How to be Taller" by Stan Dupp.

947 "A Terrible Nightmare" by Gladys Over.

948 "Famous Frights" by Terry Fied.

949 "Strong Winds" by Gail Forse.

950 "Swimming the English Channel" by Frances Neer.

951 "World Atlas" by Joe Graffie.

952 "Speaking French" by Lorna Lang Wedge.

953 "Close Shaves" by Ray Zerr.

954 "Great Eggspectations" by Charles Chickens.

955 "How to be Shorter" by Neil Down.

956 "Rice Growing" by Paddy Field.

957 "Horror Stories" by R. U. Scared.

958 "Up the Amazon" by P. Rhana.

959 "The Unknown Author" by Anne Onymous.

960 "The Long Walk to School" by Mr. Bus.

961 "Infectious Diseases" by Willie Catchit.

962 "Exercise At Home" by Ben Dan Stretch.

963 "A Bullfighter's Life" by Matt Adore.

964 "Broken Window" by Eva Brick.

965 "The Mad Cat" by Claud Boddy.

966 "Egyptian Mummies" by M. Barmer.

967 "Hungry Dog" by Nora Bone.

968 "A Hole in the Bucket" by Lee King.

969 "Camping in Iceland" by I. C. Blast.

970 "The Poltergeist" by Eve L. Spirit.

971 "A Ghost in the Attic" by Howie Wales.

972 "Explosives for Beginners" by Dinah Might.

973 "Ghosts and Ghouls" by Sue Pernatural.

974 "The Omen" by B. Warned.

975 "Famous People" by Hugh Did-Watt.

976   "Clairvoyance Made Easy" by I. C. Spooks.

977   "Sahara Journey" by Rhoda Camel.

978   "Jail Break" by Freida Prizner.

979   "The Arctic Ocean" by I.C. Waters.

980 "The Haunted House" by Hugo First.

981 "Stormy Day" by A. Pauline Weather.

982 "Dealing With Bullies" by Howard U. Lykett.

983 "The Millionaire" by Iva Fortune.

984 "Easy Money" by Robin Banks.

985 "Roof Repairs" by Lee King.

986 "A Sting in the Tale" by B. Keeper.

987 "The Rainforest" by Teresa Green.

988 "Across the African Plains" by Ann T. Lope.

989 "Quick Snacks" by Roland Butter.

990 "Crossing Roads Safely" by Luke Bothways.

Vehicles

991 **W**hat happened to the wooden car with wooden wheels and a wooden engine?

It wooden go.

This one's a real beauty ... made from sustainable forests too! It's got everything! Solid timber construction full wood interior ... 4 good wheels and .... by the look of it .... TERMITES

992 **W**hat did the traffic light say to the car?

Don't look now, I'm changing.

993 **W**hat flies and wobbles?

A jellycopter.

994 **W**hy can't a bicycle stand up?

Because it's two tired.

995 **W**hen is a car not a car?

When it turns into a garage.

996 **W**hat's a fjord?

A Norwegian car.

997 **W**hat do you give a sick car?

A fuel injection.

998 **H**ow can you find a lost train?

Follow its tracks.

999 **W**hat kind of car did Elvis drive?

A Rock-n-Rolls Royce.

1000 Policeman: Did you know that you were driving at 120 mph?

Driver: Impossible. I've only been in the car for five minutes.

1001 **W**hat do you call an expensive car with a cheap name?

A poor-sche.